KEEP
CALM

AND

DRINK
UP

Andrews McMeel Publishing, LLC
an Andrews McMeel Universal company
1130 Walnut Street, Kansas City, Missouri 64106

www.andrewsmcmeel.com

13 14 15 TEN 10 9 8 7 6 5 4

ISBN: 978-1-4494-0938-8

Library of Congress Control Number: 2011923007

Published by arrangement with Summersdale Publishers Ltd.

ATTENTION: SCHOOLS AND BUSINESSES

Andrews McMeel books are available at quantity discounts with bulk purchase for educational, business, or sales promotional use. For information, please e-mail the Andrews McMeel Publishing Special Sales Department: specialsales@amuniversal.com

KEEP
CALM
AND
DRINK
UP

Andrews McMeel
Publishing, LLC
Kansas City · Sydney · London

My rule of life prescribed
as an absolutely sacred rite
smoking cigars and also the
drinking of alcohol before,
after and if need be during
all meals and in the intervals
between them.

Winston Churchill

The British have a
remarkable talent for
keeping calm, even
when there is
no crisis.

Franklin P. Jones

What two ideas are more inseparable than Beer and Britannia?

Sydney Smith

There comes a time in every woman's life when the only thing that helps is a glass of champagne.

Bette Davis

All the great villainies of
history, from the murder
of Abel to the Treaty of
Versailles, have been
perpetuated by sober men,
and chiefly by teetotalers.

H. L. Mencken

The light music of
whiskey falling into a
glass—an agreeable
interlude.

James Joyce

Good wine is a good
familiar creature if it
be well used.

William Shakespeare, *Othello*

Claret is the liquor for boys; port, for men; but he who aspires to be a hero . . . must drink brandy.

Samuel Johnson

Beer is proof that God loves
us and wants us to
be happy.

Benjamin Franklin

I know the truth is in
between the first and
fortieth drink.

Tori Amos

It is well to remember that there are five reasons for drinking: the arrival of a friend, one's present or future thirst, the excellence of the wine, or any other reason.

Latin proverb

Be happy. It's one way
of being wise.

Sidonie-Gabrielle Colette

The problem with
some people is that
when they aren't
drunk, they're sober.

W. B. Yeats

In 1969 I gave up women
and alcohol: it was the worst
twenty minutes of my life.

George Best

Wine is a living
liquid containing no
preservatives.

Julia Child

Beer is the reason I get out
of bed every afternoon.

Anonymous

You are not drunk if you can lie on the floor without holding on.

Dean Martin

I'm not a heavy drinker; I can sometimes go for hours without touching a drop.

Noël Coward

I tried to drown my sorrows,
but the bastards learned
how to swim, and now I am
overwhelmed by this decent
and good feeling.

Frida Kahlo

Ale, man, ale's the
stuff to drink
For fellows whom it
hurts to think.

A. E. Housman, *A Shropshire Lad*

The healthiest and
most health-giving
of drinks.

Louis Pasteur on wine

Twenty-four hours in a day,
twenty-four beers in a case.
Coincidence?

Stephen Wright

Remember: "i" before "e," except in Budweiser.

Anonymous

Always do sober what you said you'd do drunk. That will teach you to keep your mouth shut.

Ernest Hemingway

You are only young once, but you can be immature for a lifetime.

John P. Grier

Give strong drink unto him
that is ready to perish, and
wine unto those that be of
heavy hearts. Let him drink,
and forget his poverty, and
remember his misery
no more.

Proverbs 31:6

Wine is bottled poetry.

Robert Louis Stevenson

The greatest invention in the history of mankind is beer . . . the wheel was also a fine invention, but the wheel does not go nearly as well with pizza.

Dave Barry

I feel sorry for people who don't drink. When they wake up in the morning, that's as good as they're going to feel all day.

Frank Sinatra

If you are irritated
by every rub, how
will your mirror be
polished?

Rumi

I drink too much. The last
time I gave a urine sample it
had an olive in it.

Rodney Dangerfield

I am drinking the stars!

**Dom Pérignon on his first sip
of champagne**

I should never have
switched from scotch
to martinis.

Humphrey Bogart's last words

Rule number one is, don't sweat the small stuff. Rule number two is, it's all small stuff.

Robert Eliot

It pays to get drunk
with the best people.

Joe E. Lewis

Only Irish coffee provides
in a single glass all four
essential food groups:
alcohol, caffeine, sugar,
and fat.

Alex Levine

What contemptible
scoundrel has stolen
the cork to my lunch?

W. C. Fields

There are only two times I
drink beer: when I'm alone
and when I'm with
someone else.

Anonymous

I like to drink martinis.
Two, at the most.
Three, I'm under the table;
Four, I'm under the host.

Dorothy Parker

For every storm,
a calm,
For every thirst,
a beer.

Anonymous

Good company,
good wine, good
welcome, can make
good people.

William Shakespeare, *Henry VIII*

You can't be a real country
unless you have a
beer . . . it helps if you
have some kind of a
football team, or some
nuclear weapons . . . at the
very least you need a beer.

Frank Zappa

Responsible drinking?
Now that's an
oxymoron.

Aaron Howard

Good cognac is like a woman. Do not assault it. Coddle and warm it in your hands before you sip it.

Winston Churchill

I drink therefore I am.

W. C. Fields

Quaintest thoughts—
queerest fancies
Come to life and fade away;
What care I how time
advances?
I am drinking ale today.

Edgar Allan Poe

Good God! I've never drunk
a vintage that starts with a
number two before.

Nicholas Soames

Good wine is a
necessity of life
for me.

Thomas Jefferson

If merely feeling good could decide, drunkenness would be the supremely valid human experience.

William James

In victory, you deserve champagne; in defeat, you need it.

Napoleon Bonaparte

When alchemists first
learned how to distill spirits,
they called it *aqua vitae*, the
water of life . . . they thought
the discovery was divinely
inspired.

Gene Logsdon, *Good Spirits*

What whiskey will not cure, there is no cure for.

Irish proverb

Rum, n.: Generically, fiery liquors that produce madness in total abstainers.

Ambrose Bierce

It takes only one drink to get
me drunk. The trouble is,
I can't remember if it's the
thirteenth or the fourteenth.

George F. Burns

When I read about
the evils of drinking, I
gave up reading.

Henny Youngman

If I had my life to live over,
I would perhaps have more
actual troubles, but I'd have
fewer imaginary ones.

Don Herold

If you resolve to give up smoking, drinking and loving, you don't actually live longer. It just seems longer.

Clement Freud

Sometimes too much
to drink is barely
enough.

Mark Twain

Beer is a wholesome liquor . . . it abounds with nourishment.

Dr. Benjamin Rush

One martini is all right. Two
are too many, and three are
not enough.

James Thurber

I never drink water;
that is the stuff that
rusts pipes.

W. C. Fields

It is immoral to get drunk
because the headache
comes after the drinking,
but if the headache came
first and the drunkenness
afterwards, it would be
moral to get drunk.

Samuel Butler

Why don't you get out
of that wet coat and
into a dry martini?

Robert Benchley

Malt does more than
Milton can
To justify God's ways
to man.

A. E. Housman, *A Shropshire Lad*

My doctor told me to watch my drinking, so now I do it in front of the mirror.

Rodney Dangerfield

Let's drink together friendly
and embrace,
That all their eyes may bear
those tokens home
Of our restored love
and amity.

**William Shakespeare, *Henry IV,
Part II***

Everybody should believe in something; I believe I'll have another drink.

Anonymous

Vodka is tasteless
going down, but it is
memorable coming up.

Garrison Keillor

The English have an
extraordinary ability
for flying into a
great calm.

Alexander Woollcott

Jameson's Irish Whiskey
really does improve with
age: the older I get the more
I like it.

Bob Monkhouse

Drink because you are
happy, but never because
you are miserable.

G. K. Chesterton

I only drink to make other people seem interesting.

George Jean Nathan

Alcohol may be man's worst
enemy, but the Bible says
love your enemy.

Frank Sinatra

I try not to drink too
much because when
I'm drunk, I bite.

Bette Midler

Gin and drugs, dear lady, gin and drugs.

T. S. Eliot, when asked about inspiration

Is the glass half full, or half empty? It depends on whether you're pouring, or drinking.

Bill Cosby

Drinking beer doesn't make
you fat, it makes you lean
. . . against bars, tables,
chairs, and poles.

Anonymous

Wine gives a man
nothing . . . it only
puts in motion what
had been locked up
in frost.

Samuel Johnson

Do not cease to drink beer, to eat, to intoxicate thyself, to make love, and to celebrate the good days.

Ancient Egyptian proverb

Drunkenness is nothing but voluntary madness.

Seneca

Alcohol removes
inhibitions—like that scared
little mouse who got drunk
and shook his whiskers and
shouted: "Now bring on
that damn cat!"

Eleanor Early

There's naught, no
doubt, so much the
spirit calms as rum
and true religion.

Lord Byron

If four or five guys tell you
that you're drunk, even
though you know you
haven't had a thing to drink,
the least you can do is to lie
down a little while.

Joseph Schenck

Wine is sunlight, held
together by water.

Galileo

Be like a duck. Calm on the surface, but always paddling like the dickens underneath.

Michael Caine

If you keep on
drinking rum, the
world will soon be
quit of a very dirty
scoundrel.

Robert Louis Stevenson

He was a wise man
who invented beer.

Plato

For art to exist, for any
sort of aesthetic activity or
perception to exist, a certain
physiological precondition is
indispensable: intoxication.

Friedrich Nietzsche

I drink no more than
a sponge.

François Rabelais

The water was not fit to drink. To make it palatable, we had to add whiskey. By diligent effort, I learned to like it.

Winston Churchill

This is one of the
disadvantages of wine; it
makes a man mistake words
for thoughts.

Samuel Johnson

God has a brown
voice, as soft and full
as beer.

Anne Sexton

What soberness
conceals, drunkenness
reveals.

Proverb

Alcohol may not solve your problems, but neither will water or milk.

Anonymous

An intelligent man is
sometimes forced to be
drunk to spend time with
his fools.

Ernest Hemingway

Work is the curse of
the drinking classes.

Oscar Wilde

A drink a day keeps
the shrink away.

Edward Abbey

If you ever reach total enlightenment while drinking beer, I bet it makes beer shoot out your nose.

Jack Handy

Wine rejoices the heart of man and joy is the mother of all virtues.

Johann Wolfgang von Goethe

The pub knows a lot,
almost as much as
the churches.

Joyce Carey

Alcohol is the anesthesia
by which we endure the
operation of life.

George Bernard Shaw

An alcoholic is anyone
you don't like who
drinks as much as
you do.

Dylan Thomas

Red wine is just like ketchup: it goes with everything.

Jason Walton

I think hangovers are the body's way of telling us we didn't drink enough to still be drunk when we woke up the next day.

Anonymous

On some days, my head
is filled with such wild and
original thoughts that I can
barely utter a word. On other
days, the liquor store
is closed.

Frank Varano

It's a long time
between drinks.

Robert Browning

Beer makes you feel the
way you ought to feel
without beer.

Henry Lawson

Happiness never decreases by being shared.

Buddha

Abstainer, n.: A weak person who yields to the temptation of denying himself a pleasure.

Ambrose Bierce

Drink moderately, for drunkenness neither keeps a secret, nor observes a promise.

Miguel de Cervantes

The chief reason for drinking
is the desire to behave in a
certain way, and to be able
to blame it on alcohol.

Mignon McLaughlin

I am a drinker with writing problems.

Brendan Behan

Wine gives courage
and makes men more
apt for passion.

Ovid

You can always retake a
class, but you can never
relive a party.

Drew Navikas

My grandmother is over eighty and still doesn't need glasses. Drinks right out of the bottle.

Henny Youngman

We borrowed golf from Scotland as we borrowed whiskey. Not because it is Scottish, but because it is good.

Horace Hutchinson

There can be nothing more frequent than an occasional drink.

Oscar Wilde

I used to have a
drinking problem. Now
I love the stuff.

Anonymous

He who seldom speaks, and with one calm, well-timed word can strike dumb the loquacious, is a genius or a hero.

Johann Kaspar Lavater

I've never been drunk,
but often I've been
overserved.

George Gobel

Drinking spirits
cannot cause spiritual
damage.

José Bergamín

It's better to light a candle
than to curse the darkness.

Eleanor Roosevelt

Man, being reasonable,
must get drunk; the best of
life is but intoxication.

Lord Byron

Beer that is not drunk has missed its vocation.

Meyer Breslau

Do not allow children
to mix drinks. It
is unseemly and
they use too much
vermouth.

Steve Allen

Alcohol is like love: the first kiss is magic, the second is intimate, the third is routine. After that you just take the girl's clothes off.

Raymond Chandler

A meal without wine is like
a day without sunshine,
except that on a day without
sunshine you can still get
drunk.

Lee Entrekin

The trouble with jogging is that the ice falls out of your glass.

Martin Mull

Be wary of strong drink. It can make you shoot at tax collectors and miss.

Robert Heinlein

He occasionally takes
an "alcoholiday."

Oscar Wilde

There is no joy
but calm!

**Lord Alfred Tennyson,
"The Lotus Eaters"**

Not all chemicals are bad. Without . . . hydrogen and oxygen . . . there would be no way to make water, a vital ingredient in beer.

Dave Barry

My dad was the town drunk. Most of the time that's not so bad, but New York City?

Henny Youngman

No animal ever invented
anything so bad as
drunkenness—or so good
as drink.

G. K. Chesterton

Reality is an illusion created
by a lack of alcohol.

Anonymous

There can't be good
living where there is
not good drinking.

Benjamin Franklin

I'm Catholic and I can't
commit suicide, but I plan to
drink myself to death.

Jack Kerouac

It is a fair wind that
blew men to the ale.

Washington Irving

But the greatest love—the
love above all loves—
Even greater than that of
a mother,
Is the tender, passionate,
undying love,
Of one beer-drunken slob
for another.

Irish proverb

I think a man ought
to get drunk at least
twice a year just on
principle, so he won't
let himself get snotty
about it.

Raymond Chandler

Champagne, if you
are seeking the truth,
is better than a
lie detector.

Graham Greene

Even though a number of people have tried, no one has yet found a way to drink for a living.

Jean Kerr

Whenever you are sincerely pleased, you are nourished.

Ralph Waldo Emerson

The proper union of gin and vermouth is a great and sudden glory; it is one of the happiest marriages on earth, and one of the shortest lived.

Bernard DeVoto

I only take a drink on two occasions: when I'm thirsty and when I'm not.

Brendan Behan

Great events make
me quiet and calm;
it is only trifles that
irritate my nerves.

Queen Victoria

Let us have wine and
women, mirth and laughter,
Sermons and soda water
the day after.

Lord Byron

Milk is for babies.
When you grow up you
have to drink beer.

Arnold Schwarzenegger

Champagne is the
only wine that leaves
a woman beautiful
after drinking it.

Madame de Pompadour

Always remember that I
have taken more out of
alcohol than alcohol has
taken out of me.

Winston Churchill

Be glad of life because it gives you the chance to love, to work, to play, and to look up at the stars.

Henry Van Dyke

Always be drunk . . .
Get drunk militantly.
Just get drunk.

Charles Baudelaire

Drinking is a way of ending the day.

Ernest Hemingway

You only live once, but if you
do it right, once is enough.

Mae West